The Santa Barbara Bargain Book

The Santa Barbara Bargain Book

SHOP 'TIL YOU DROP WITHOUT GOING BROKE

Cheri Rae

Pacific Books
SANTA BARBARA

*Dedicated to the Santa Barbara
shopkeepers and restaurateurs
who strive to provide an
alternative to Anywhere, U.S.A.*

Book Design and Typography: Jim Cook
Cover Design: Deja Hsu
Editorial Services: Olympus Press
Printer: Bill McNally, Kimberly Press

The author gratefully extends her thanks to the following individuals who assisted in the creation of this book: To Steve
Hoegerman and Francess Lantz for providing a taste of the
town; to my sister-in-shopping Jane M. Reisman for suggestions and encouragement; to Anna Raye Clarke for blazing the
Santa Barbara bargain trail; to Michael Zolkoski, go-getter
bookseller who championed this book from the word go; to
John McKinney, who hiked out of the wilderness to help me
navigate through the low-priced paseos.

Published & Distributed by
Pacific Books
P.O. Box 3562
Santa Barbara, California 93130
(805) 687-8340

Contents

Introduction

I love finding a bargain—just about everyone does. I find bargains whenever, wherever I travel, and I find them at home in Santa Barbara. But bargains in Santa Barbara are few and far between, or so the image goes.

Santa Barbara is known as a playground of the rich and famous, an idyllic slice of Mediterranean life on the Pacific. Most visitors take one look at the pricey façade and think to themselves, "It's a nice place to visit but I wouldn't want to shop there."

What's not commonly known about this city, however, is that it is a bargain-hunter's paradise—if you know where to look. This book is your passport to Santa Barbara's world of consignment shops and vintage clothing stores, to factory outlets and discounted home furnishing emporiums. With this guide you'll get more from your food dollars by shopping European-style at patisseries and produce stands, and dining at neighborhood eateries. You'll learn to stretch your entertainment dollar with freebies and bargain matinees.

The very factors that make Santa Barbara such a great place to visit—setting, climate, environment and ambience—make it a magnet for certain stylish small businesses. Artists, apparel manufacturers and other creative types flourish here, and many offer their wares to the local public at reduced prices.

I didn't realize the size and scope of such local enterprises until I wrote a story for the *Los Angeles Times* about factory outlet shopping in Santa Barbara. Researching the piece, I was amazed to find a dozen such outlets in my hometown. Reader response was enthusiastic. Shoppers still wander into outlets clutching that tattered newspaper article clipped from the *Times* a few years ago.

Publication of that piece coincided with the onset of the recession. And since then, times have really changed. The second-worst fire in California's history blazed through America's Riviera causing nearly a billion dollars worth of damage. A Santa Barbara city councilman resorted to switching price tags at a local home improvement center; public furor forced him to resign, but privately many sympathized with his frustration at the high prices charged locally. As the '90s progressed, even "Santa Barbara," the soap opera, was cancelled.

Increasingly, the arrogance of those ignoring current economic conditions—the shopkeeper unblinkingly offering a $5,000 silk comforter, the realtor calling a $438,900 listing "a mere pittance"—comes across not merely as irrelevant, but actually as insulting to anyone who knows the value of a dollar and the way people really live.

Our lingering recession means that just about everyone, everywhere—even in Santa Barbara—has to allocate their dollars in creative ways. I don't know about you, but recession or not, I'm not about to become an uptight tightwad, madly saving pickle juice and collecting the lint from my clothes dryer, as some frugal zealots preach. I'd rather put time and energy into more pleasurable bargain-hunting pursuits.

And that's what this book is about: Finding the best value for the money spent. For visitors it means stepping off the tourist track and onto less traveled roads; for locals it means cancelling those out-of-town shopping trips and finding deals right here at home. For visitors and locals alike it means bypassing the well-advertised specialty chains and department stores in favor of smaller, locally owned shops that offer original inventories and personalized services.

Above all, this book is about having fun with the shopping experience. It's about discovering new places, meeting interesting people, finding a few terrific deals, and enjoying Santa Barbara in an entirely new way.

Clothing

Lots of us derive exquisite pleasure from the entire process of shopping for clothes—dressing up, enjoying the sociable atmosphere, looking for the best deal, searching for just the right pieces that make a statement.

The wonderful little secret about shopping for clothes in Santa Barbara is that it is possible to shop 'til you drop without going broke.

The trick is to avoid the big department stores, the national chains and chi-chi boutiques—at least until you've checked out all the wonderful alternatives, namely consignment, vintage and resale shops. There are lots of them around, most well stocked with quality, brand-name merchandise and interesting clothes that set the wearer apart from the crowd.

Consignment Shops

Santa Barbara's consignment shops have very high standards, and a loyal following—let's face it, Beautiful People with Big Bucks didn't get rich by giving away their pricey threads—they just, er, recycle them in Santa Barbara's consignment shops.

This is how they work: consignors bring clothing and accessories to the shops, which then offer selected items for sale to the general public. When items are sold, the shop typically splits the purchase price 50/50 with the consignor—and the buyer gets a great deal on a designer fashion.

The clothing sold in consignment shops is usually in excellent condition (some items are brand-new, most have been worn only a few times). Remember, though, that a bargain in high-fashion designer wear may still be pricey, and buying even at a fraction of retail will cost you. But look at it this way, where else are you going to have the opportunity to buy Armani at Liz Claiborne prices?

Autumn's Uptown

1429 State Street
965-5215
Monday-Saturday 10-5

Autumn's Uptown, established in 1981, has developed a loyal clientele over the years—both in shoppers and consignors. This truly uptown shop features "exclusive designer fashions at a fraction of original cost." Browse through the racks of this shop and you know you're looking at elegant clothing—ranging from sportswear to career suits and evening wear—that has previously hung in Santa Barbara's finest closets.

On a given day the selection may include top labels including Armani, Cascadi, Escada, Oscar de la Renta and more. This is one of the few shops in town that carries men's wear: it's a small rack featuring mostly top-quality designs by Armani, Hugo Boss and others. A nice selection of Italian shoes, jewelry and fine accessories are also priced well below retail.

Clothing

Jessica

2012 De La Vina Street
867-2755
Monday-Saturday 10-5; Saturday 11-5:30
Jessica features a variety of designer and fine women's apparel and accessories, ranging from a simple Jessica McClintock dress to a Moschino couture linen jacket. We're talking high-end merchandise at affordable prices. If you've dreamed of wearing a DKNY silk bodysuit, this is the place you may find at—and still be able to make your next car payment. This is a very popular shop with a very comfortable atmosphere. Check out the sale rack out front, and the small selection of interesting jewelry.

Lillian's Consignments

3400 State Street
563-1226
Monday-Friday 10-5:30; Saturday 10-5
The professional woman can find an entire wardrobe here—from dressy to casual—with all the accessories to match. From fur-trimmed and mink coats to jersey top with leggings, it's quality clothing at affordable prices. Owner Lillian O'Toole confides that many of her customers have experienced big changes in their lives—weight loss or weight gain, a new job in a different field—and they need lots of new clothes fast, without paying a fortune for them. Designer labels may include Umberto Ginocchietti, Rafael, Escada, and more; look for a great selection of pricey Dooney & Bourke bags at less than half-price.

Nita's Boutique

113 West Mission Street
569-1750
Tuesday-Saturday 10-5:30
Catering primarily to a clientele of professional women of all ages at work and at play, the shop's motto is "We cater to ladies who want to look like a million on someone else's million."

You may find an Escada suit at one-third original price, and less pricey items from Anne Klein, Carole Little and Liz Claiborne. This is the only consignment shop in town to stock a big selection of wedding gowns (some worn once, others never worn), bridesmaids' dresses in multiple, and a number of mother-of-the-bride dresses. Poke through the baskets of $1 costume jewelry, and examine the shoes and handbags on display. For more shopping tips, pick up a copy of the brochure, "How to Shop Resale," prepared by the National Association of Resale and Thrift Shops (Nita's is a member).

Play it Again Sam
10 East Carrillo Street
966-9989
Monday-Saturday 10-6; Sunday 12-5

Contemporary clothing for a casual lifestyle is featured at Play it Again Sam. Labels here include Laura Ashley, Ann Taylor and Contempo; you'll find a great selection of party dresses at prom time and during the holiday season. There's a rack of previously owned leotards and swimsuits, and a great selection of new accessories, especially hats, hair accessories, socks and tights.

This is the place to buy sterling silver jewelry; it's almost always on special: buy one piece, get the second piece at one-half off.

Redesigning Women
3530 State Street
687-1309
Monday-Saturday 11-6

Redesigning Women caters to established professional women with tastes ranging from classic to current: St. John knits, DKNY and Lanz are a few of the labels favored. The selection includes suits, evening clothes and sportswear. This is one of the newer shops in town, but it's already built up a loyal clientele, due in large part to the shop's philosophy: "If it doesn't look like new, then it shouldn't be re-sold." Look for a nice selection of jewelry, some shoes and handbags.

Rosebud Boutique Consignment
3024 De La Vina Street
682-4820
Tuesday-Friday 11-4; Saturday 10-5
This elegantly appointed shop, complete with antique chairs and crafted mirrors, houses "haute couture for the smart, sleek sophisticate." Believe it. The designer originals carried here include Bill Blass, Nino Cerruti, Christian Dior, Ralph Lauren, Anne Klein and more. There's a large selection of suits, a rack of fantasy formalwear, lots of silks and wools. The back room contains an assortment of casual wear, jeans, blouses, jackets, sweaters and skirts. Owner June Rachal Travolta (yes, stepmother of John *Saturday Night Fever* Travolta) caters to a steady clientele of women with sophisticated taste, and especially enjoys providing personalized service.

Vintage Clothing

Santa Barbara has long supported a group of distinctive vintage clothing shops, and has recently welcomed a number of newcomers. These shops are now located within just a couple of blocks of each other—great for an afternoon full of shopping discoveries.

The great thing about wearing vintage clothes—items that are so obviously from another time, be it Victorian, '30s, '50s or '60s—is that they almost invariably attract attention and compliments—far more than the basic department store stuff everybody else is wearing. You don't have to go all out with an entire outfit; just a piece here and there—sweater, Hawaiian shirt, classic jeans, a great tie or period piece of jewelry can really snazz up a look at a great price.

Drama

15 East Ortega Street

963-1217

Monday-Saturday 11-6; Sunday 12-5

This mother-daughter business opened in October 1992, after Marie and Sara Prevedello purchased the inventory of a Hollywood studio. The nostalgic clothing from the '30s, '40s and '50s is enough to make you swoon. The looks are right out of the movies, and every item is tagged with the name of an appropriate star, character, movie or television show.

Slip on a pair of "I Love Lucy" houndstooth capris, a "Lana Turner" linen and beaded dress, a "William Holden" or a "Clark Kent" suit, and you'll feel like you stepped off the silver screen.

The shop features imaginative displays, period post cards, music and videos, with a great selection of collectibles, linens, costume jewelry and wonderful hats.

Max Ballard

21 West Ortega Street
966-9006
Monday-Saturday 10-6; Sunday 12-5

Max Ballard carries an eclectic assortment of clothing styles, specializing primarily in bikinis and junior wear. This is not technically a vintage shop, but the buyers have located a couple of vintage suppliers that market a line of "recycled clothing." Here you'll find cleaned-up, lace-embellished jackets, vests and shirts at about half regular retail price.

Pure Gold

625 State Street
962-4613
Monday-Saturday 10-6; Sunday 12-6

A poster on the wall says it all: "Wink at Tradition."

Owner Julia Huffman started Pure Gold fifteen years ago. "I've always loved old stuff and hand-me-downs," she said. The shop is stocked with quality clothing in good condition, all clean and mended, from sources all over the country.

Browse through the racks and you'll find everything from a demure nightgown, circa 1910 to psychedelic print mini-dresses straight out of the '60s. About a quarter of Pure Gold's inventory is menswear, and they also offer a selection of period linens, accessories—hats, gloves and jewelry—and the greatest assortment of new Doc Martens this side of Los Angeles.

Rags to Riches/Something Old, Something New

35 East Ortega Street
966-1171 / 966-5500
Monday-Saturday 11-5; call for Sunday hours

This location houses two shops: Rags to Riches specializes in vintage clothing, jewelry and art; Something Old, Something New (as the name suggests) handles vintage and original bridal fashions.

Rags to Riches owner Rosemary Pelli purchases virtually all of her inventory in New York—at church sales, yard sales and estate sales, and from individuals she meets along the way. "The steamy smell of old trunks excites me," she enthuses.

Linger in this shop and look around; the treasures aren't always immediately apparent, but they range from lingerie to formal gowns, in styles from Victorian to contemporary. Rely on Rosemary to tell you about the background of virtually every item she offers for sale.

Upstairs from Rags to Riches is a romantic little find: Something Old, Something New. Ascending the satin-backed stairway feels like climbing up to Grandma's attic. The tiny shop is a wonder of romantic gowns, headpieces and accessories; it's all appointed in white lace and old wicker. Shopowner/fashion designer Kareen Hart offers a range of designs fashioned in linen, satin and cotton, in styles from sweet Victorian to sleek contemporary. She's collected vintage lace and fashions for years, and puts both her interest and skills to work fashioning custom headpieces, reproductions of period dresses, and restoring old lace. Is your heart set on wearing Grandmother's antique lace dress to your own wedding? This is the place to make your dream come true. Hours by appointment only.

Tekla
11 West Ortega Street
LOV-1967
Monday-Saturday 10-6; Sunday 12-6

The shop's motto is "Strange stuff and a few normal things." And that just about sums it up. Owner Sandi Ramundt, who previously supplied period clothing for movies (*JFK* and *The Doors*) and television ("Quantum Leap"), opened Tekla in October 1992 after she relocated from Los Angeles. The shop specializes in the distinctive styles from the '60s and '70s, although you'll find select items from earlier decades as well.

Hip huggers and hot pants, embroidered work shirts, platforms and crushed velvet coats—everything that used to hang in your closet (or your parents' closet) is available here. Enjoy the period music, lounge on the leopard chaise and soak up the atmosphere of shoppers discovering—or rediscovering—the fun of fashion.

True Grit

37 East Ortega Street
564-1355
Monday-Saturday 11-6; Sunday 12-5

If you live your life in the wide-open spaces of the Great American West (or if you just wish you did), True Grit—and its line of Vintage American Classics—is the place for you. The rustic shop is filled with broken-in cowboy boots, belt buckles, Levi 501s, blanket vests and jean jackets.

This is one of the few shops anywhere you can find collectible Levi's—jeans and jackets manufactured pre-1971. How can you tell? The little red tag on the pocket has a capital "E" in the word "Levi's." In those days, the manufacturer used real indigo dye and cut the jeans for a relaxed fit. Like just about everything else from our happy hippie days, they're worth big bucks—like $200 a pair!

Check out its inexpensive and very unique bandanna wrap mini-skirts, overalls and turquoise jewelry. You'll go from city slicker to ranch hand quicker 'n you can say "Howdy, pardner."

Victorian Vogue & The Costume Shoppe

13 West Ortega Street
962-8824
Monday-Thursday 11-6; Friday-Saturday 10-6; Sunday 12-6

There's always a $5 sale rack outside, a $15 sale rack inside, and window displays that entice you to step in—and what surprises await you! The place is stuffed to the rafters with a colorful mix of clothing representing every imaginable style and time period.

The shop is a combination of vintage clothing, contemporary formal and casual wear, and wild costumes for every dress-up occasion. "Everything is for sale or rent," quipped one clerk, "except the cash register." While one customer rents a medieval gown to wear to a Renaissance Faire, another examines crystal necklaces and cameos to give as a gift, and yet another searches the formal rack to rent a vintage tux to wear at his wedding. Wonderful hats, jewelry and the only white go-go boots in town.

Plan ahead: customers are lined up outside the door before major Santa Barbara holidays: Solstice, Fiesta and Halloween.

Yellowstone
527 State Street
963-9609
Monday-Saturday 10-6; Sunday 11-5

This is the shop for great beaded sweaters, Hawaiian shirts, bowling shirts and '40s ties, along with Levi 501s (the shop's largest selling item), men's jackets and beautiful kimonos.

Owners Stephanie and Paul Haugen have been in the business nearly twenty years, and they know their stuff. They carry items from the '30s to current fashions, and enjoy a steady stream of loyal customers, including many visitors who make their annual stop in the shop. The clothes are a great draw, and so are the linens: chenille bedspreads, quilts, souvenir tableclothes and crocheted doilies and dresser scarves. If unique is what you seek, stop here first.

Resale Clothing

Resale shops typically scour for goods everywhere they can. Some take donations, others arrange for trades or pay for goods outright. Whatever. The important point is that it's available for sale to you—usually at lower prices than you might typically find at consignment shops, and by design, more current fashions than you would find at vintage shops.

Blue Moon Exchange

5122 Hollister Avenue
Goleta
967-0610
Monday-Saturday 10-6

Located in Magnolia Shopping Center, this shop stocks mostly lower-priced previously owned and new junior wear.

Lots of labels from The Limited and Contempo; Gitano, Big Dogs and other sportswear. Extensive selection of low-cost accessories for the hair, costume jewelry, belts and some shoes.

The Rack

Music Academy of the West
73 Butterfly Lane
Montecito
969-0190
Tuesday-Saturday 1-4

The clothing found at The Rack has been donated by auxiliary members and friends of the Music Academy of the West. Sales at the tiny shop, located on the grounds of the academy, are earmarked for student scholarships. Look for high-quality designer labels including Escada and Scaasi at well below retail price. The annual May Madness sale is a grand affair, and a must-attend for dedicated shoppers. The Rack's high-end resale items are offered, along with men's wear and new clothing donated by several Santa Barbara shops—all at great savings.

19

Ragz

501 Chapala Street
962-8808
Monday-Saturday 12-6

Housed in a huge pink Victorian (the one-time home of the Stearns family as in Stearns Wharf) that is located on a busy corner, this shop is impossible to miss—and that's good, because it's a must-visit bargain shop. Owner Maywor Mansson has a great time with this place, and it shows. "Experienced clothing worth repeating" is the phrase she's coined to characterize her inventory, and it's an apt description.

The up-to-date clothes are mostly arranged by color, some by style. There are plenty of designer and fashionable labels to be found—Guess, Henri Grethel, Ann Taylor, WilliWear, Joan & David, Bis, Gap—all at very affordable prices. Don't miss the great selection of silk scarves, hats and linen shirts. I couldn't resist an impeccable asymmetrically cut Issey Miyake linen shirt for $18!

Clothing

Kid's Stuff

There are so many adorable children's clothes available today, that you could really go crazy—and quite broke—outfitting your little one in all the latest fashions. Because kids of all ages grow so fast and are so hard on their clothes, buying them recycled wear makes a lot of sense. Wonderful surprises are out there, but like a lot of bargain shopping, you may have to be persistent and sort through a lot of not-so-nice pieces to find what you like. Number one hint: visit these shops early and often. The best items—in terms of quality and price—go fast!

Cheeks/The Baby Exchange
1819 Cliff Drive
568-1930
Monday-Saturday 10-6:30; Sunday 11-5
(At press time, owner Linda Martin was frantically looking for a new location for her shop; call before visit.) This no-frills shop gets down to basics: lots of clothes, toys, books, and all the stuff you need for kids. It's a great place to recycle the clothes your little tykes have outgrown, and stock up on bigger sizes they'll outgrow next. A small selection of maternity wear, baby furniture, car seats and carriers of all sorts.

Cotton Club
1921-B De La Vina Street
687-1512
Tuesday-Saturday 10:30-4:30
This tiny shop is crammed full of mostly used clothing for infants and children, along with an extensive selection of maternity wear. There are some locally manufactured items including colorful stuffed dolphin toys and tie-dyed T-shirts.

Polar Bear

726 Anacapa Street
965-6637
Monday-Saturday 10-5; Sunday 11-5
A little funky, located in a corrugated steel building. Low prices on good quality new clothing, particularly shoes, pajamas and rompers. Used selection varies in quality, but some good deals can be found on overalls, corduroy pants and sometimes party dresses. Sizes infant to 14. Adjacent room has used baby furnishings (strollers, port-a-cribs, etc.) at decent prices.

Twice Upon a Time

11 West Anapamu Street
962-1884
Monday-Saturday 10-5:30; Sunday 12-5
Located just around the corner from Earthling Bookshop, the wonderful display window of this shop offers a hint of what's inside. Charming flowered prints, unique and trendy designs in new and gently worn clothing from infants to school-age. The atmosphere is enchanting, with hand-painted furniture, books, unique toys and musical instruments. You'll finds some great bargains on the sale rack of past-season's clothes; pick up a monthly calendar filled with special (and often whimsically inspired) daily discounts.

Browse through the "Marketplace for Munchkins," a notebook filled with ads for equipment—furniture, strollers, cribs and the like—for sale by private parties.

Jewelry

The Family Jewels
716 State Street
965-6654
Monday-Thursday and Saturday 10-6; Friday 10-7; Sunday 12-5

"Everybody in Santa Barbara is rich," said owner Estelle Karp with a wry smile. "That's what everybody always tells me." She, like most of us, knows better. That's why Karp, along with her husband David take at least 25 percent off the manufacturers' list price of everything they sell (except Casio and Lorus watches). That includes wedding trios, pendants and several name-brand watches, including Seiko, Bulova, Citizen and Pulsar. Gold, sold by weight, is all at least 14 karat, and sold at one-third manufacturers' list price. Full low-cost repair services available on the premises; the staff speaks Spanish.

Home & Garden

In Southern California, particularly Santa Barbara with its notoriously high housing prices, the American Dream of owning a home sometimes seems more like the Impossible Dream. Problem is, once you've scraped together enough money to get your own place, how can you afford to decorate it?

Whether home is rented, mortgaged or otherwise, and if your tastes are eclectic, you might furnish it just the way you like it by shopping at some or all of the following establishments. It may take a little work—from persistence in seeking out bargains to refinishing furniture, with lots of imagination in between but it might just be worth it. One-of-a-kind, well-built, classic and unusual pieces, along with traditionally elegant furnishings are all available at well-below original prices.

The following finds offer interesting alternatives to the traditional department or furniture store route to home decor. (Note: The Factory Outlet chapter also includes several shops that carry items for home and garden.)

Home Furnishings

Garrett's Clearance Center

4188 Carpinteria Avenue
Carpinteria
684-4849
Tuesday-Friday 10-4

One-of-a-kind merchandise, floor models, discontinued styles and the like are shipped here from the Garrett's showroom in Santa Barbara—resulting in great savings if you find here what you're looking for. All items, from couches to armoires, floor lamps to silver candlestick holders are sold at 50 percent off original price. This is pricey stuff at great savings. Garrett's Annual Warehouse Clearance Sale is held each spring: showroom displays, samples, slightly damaged merchandise and discontinued items are sold at 50 percent discount or more. Cash and carry only; well advertised in local papers in advance of event.

Montecito Country Consignments

1277 Coast Village Road
Montecito
969-9062
Tuesday-Sunday 12-5:30

This tiny, quite charming shop carries consigned quality furniture—chairs, tables, desks, sofas and the like—along with new gift items, and fine paintings. As the address suggests, the pieces for sale certainly didn't start out as bargains, and may still carry hefty tags, but still a fraction of original price. Don't miss the potpourri pillows, ornamental wall hangings, or, if you're in the mood for a splurge, the wonderful handmade hats almost hidden away, but definitely worth a look. (I bought an unbelievably comfortable, high-quality wicker chair here for just $45.)

Opportunity Shop

127 West Canon Perdido Street
962-7233
Monday-Friday 8-5:30; Saturday 8-5

Operating in Santa Barbara since 1925, the Opportunity Shop carries household furniture in all styles, shapes and sizes. "Better than new," reads the sign, and while that assertion is debatable, there is some high-quality merchandise for sale here at reasonable prices. The furniture is arranged by type—dressers in one room, dining room sets in another, end tables, couches, beds, and so on. On any given day you may discover a real find—a Craftsman rocker, a stand-out wicker chair or Victorian sofa. Mary Ellen McCaffrey, who owns the shop with her husband John, comments, "You can find a cross-section of the community and a little bit of everything right here in this shop." One-month layaway plan available.

The Treasure House

The Music Academy of the West
75 Butterfly Lane
Montecito
969-1744
Monday-Saturday 1-4

Located on the grounds of the prestigious Music Academy of the West, the Treasure House offers a collection of fine consigned and donated furniture, housewares, collectibles and the like. Some antiques, linens, china, crystal, framed paintings, and unusual accessories can be discovered here if you poke around a bit. The shop (as well as The Rack clothing shop next door) is situated in a fine old adobe house; sales benefit the Academy's scholarship fund. Don't miss the annual May Madness sale held on the grounds each spring.

Outdoor Furniture

Hayward's Patio Center

315 State Street
965-3563
Monday-Saturday 9-5:30; Sunday 11-5

Santa Barbara's Mediterranean climate allows residents to spend lots of at-home time outdoors—on the patio, the porch or in the garden. Hayward's Patio Center is the place to go to furnish these areas with quality items that reflect the casually elegant Santa Barbara lifestyle.

Hayward's has been in the Santa Barbara furniture biz since 1890, and they know what the people like: wooden and wrought-iron garden benches, Brown Jordan and other brands of patio furniture, colorful cushions and graceful umbrellas. Hayward's buys in huge volume and discounts virtually everything in the store, including the stylish market umbrella manufactured locally by Santa Barbara Designs. (The long list of the rich and famous who have ordered the umbrella includes Madonna, Cher and local residents Michael Douglas and Steve Martin.)

Charming outdoor accessories such as bird baths, weather vanes, baker's racks, pots and figurines are also carried here. There's something for everybody in all price ranges.

Patio Outlet Store

124 West Carrillo Street
965-4343/964-8811
Weekends 10-4; sometimes open Fridays

This is a strictly no-frills operation, 6,000 square feet of discounted patio and outdoor furniture crammed into an oversized Quonset hut. It's the outlet shop for the Pool Supply and Patio Center, located on upper State Street. Poke around the shop and you'll discover marble-topped tables, chaise lounges, stacking chairs, and market umbrellas. You won't find the pricey top brands here, but this is good quality merchandise at 20 to 50 percent off retail price. The shop is open weekends only, sometimes on Friday.

Wholesale Nurseries

Doug Knapp Nursery

909 Carlo Drive
Goleta
681-1151 (recorded information or messages only)
Friday and Saturday 9-5; Sunday 10-5

Located in what at first glance appears to be a purely residential area is Doug Knapp's huge nursery. As you stroll the grounds you'll be impressed with the dramatic view of the magnificent Santa Ynez mountains, the birdsong that fills the air, and the assortment of healthy indoor and outdoor plants that can be yours at wholesale prices. Beautiful roses, a variety of drought-resistant species, exquisite fuchsias and much more. Drive the truck, and take advantage of cash (or check) and carry deals.

Island View Nursery

4045-A Foothill Road
Carpinteria
Thursday, Friday and Saturday only 9-4
684-0496

Located on five acres of prime agricultural land in Carpinteria, this wholesale nursery is open to the public just three days a week. It's worth the drive; prices are wholesale or below on a wide selection of healthy indoor and outdoor plants and terra-cotta pottery. Wander the huge greenhouses for African violets and orchids; the shadehouses for ferns; outdoor rows of bougainvillea, giant palms and just about every other plant you can name, including drought-resistant varieties. Checks are accepted, but add 3 percent for purchases charged on a credit card.

Colorful Extras

Bannerscapes Flags & Banners

726 Reddick Avenue

969-2139

hours by appointment only

Chances are that the colorful flags and banners that you see flying gaily in the wind in many places throughout Santa Barbara (and all over the nation) were stiched up in this tiny factory. Started on a shoestring by owner Nancy Newquist-Nolan, the business now counts Knott's Berry Farm and Sears Roebuck among its regular customers. Call ahead for an appointment to become one, too. Select from festive holiday designs, whimsical patterns to reflect your business or personal interests, or commission an original design. Off-season and discontinued styles are available at half-price; make-your-own flag kits will soon be available.

Brinkerhoff Avenue

Two blocks west of the 500 block of State Street (between Cota and Haley streets) is a landmark district of Victorian homes, many of which have been turned into antique and resale shops. Shop here for fine furniture, handmade linens, crystal, gift items and whimsical accessories with a past. No great bargains are necessarily in store, but it's a pleasure to examine the wares, and to get a glimpse of the interiors of the turn-of-the-century homes on this lovely street.

Cominichi's

624 State Street

965-7917

Monday-Thursday 10-10; Friday and Saturday 10-11 p.m.; Sunday 12-6

As owner/artist Gina Comin remarks to two heavily tattooed men as she examines the merchandise they're trying to sell, "The funkier the better." This shop, located in a turn-of-the century building with a wonderful ceiling (it has housed a Mexican restaurant and served as the headquarters for the Solstice Parade), is a flea market like you've rarely seen before. The items for sale—

from vintage clothing to antique furniture—are quite amazing. Lots of '50s and '60s memorabilia, furniture, old suitcases, flower power stickers and lots more to discover. There's a poetry reading every second Thursday, and plans for swap meets on Sundays.

The Salvage Company

726 Anacapa Street
965-2446
Monday-Saturday 12-5

In the words of owner Roger Cota, "This is the place to find eclectic, weird, strange, expensive, cheap, unusual, collectible and miscellaneous stuff." Wander into this dusty, low-lit place and you'll discover his description is absolutely on-the-mark. It's full of arched windows and designer furniture, styles from antiques to modern, a wrought-iron fence here, a hi-fi there. It's a kick to rummage around and find a one-of-a-kind item that's just perfect for that corner of your home. Cota's devoted clientele travels from Los Angeles and beyond just to look around. His once-a-year ugly lamp contest (date and time known only to regulars) has become legend. If you can find what you're looking for, this place is a great bargain; even if you don't, the fun of just looking around is a deal in itself.

Sugarbush Slipcovers

33 East Victoria Street
963-8897
Monday-Friday 11-5; Saturday 11-3

Owner Barbara Blake states, "The basic concept of the business is to offer the prices of a fabric store along with the service of a decorator." Just thumb through any home magazine and you'll discover that slipcovered furniture is very popular these days. There are plenty of reasons for that popularity, not the least of which is that it's less expensive than reupholstery (or buying new furniture). Sugarbush sends an expert out to your home to take measurements and make suggestions, offers 1,000 fabric choices, and employs seamstresses to sew up the sale.

Factory Outlets

Factory outlet shopping, Santa Barbara-style, is a little different from the big discount mall-type outlet shopping that's become popular throughout the Southland—indeed, the nation. Santa Barbara's factory outlet shopping takes you not to one central location, but throughout the city, away from pricey boutiques and department stores and into the industrial and warehouse districts virtually unknown to residents and visitors alike.

Some of these outlets may be out of the way, and they may have inconvenient hours, but they provide some fun and adventurous shopping excursions. Moreover, they are clean, they offer personal service and great discounts on a wide variety of goods produced or distributed by local manufacturers. And nobody will believe you bought it wholesale—or less—in Santa Barbara!

Clothing

Big Dogs Sportswear Factory Outlet

136 State Street

963-8727

Daily 10-6

The most visible and popular factory outlet in town, this is a sportswear company with a penchant for puns and a really big dog. ("The paws that refresh," for example.) Current and past-season styles at various discounts; there's something here for every fun-loving member of the family—shorts, parkas, T-shirts and more, all featuring the lovable logo.

California Proline Factory Outlet

4 East Yanonali Street

962-5134

Monday-Saturday 10-5.

As the posters, displays, hangtags, and California Girls who staff the store make quite obvious, the teeny bikinis, tanks, leggings, sundresses and other casual wear offered here are strictly for the aerobicized junior set. Discounts begin at 25 percent off retail for first-quality in-season wear. Some items, primarily overstock, are sold at cost or just a few dollars above wholesale. These are trendy, beachy designs with a certain attitude: One advertising campaign uses the lines penned by poet Vachel Lindsay: "And the devil said to Simon Legree: I like your style, so wicked and free."

Equestrian Designs Factory Outlet

135 Nogal Drive

683-1340

Monday-Friday 8-4; for other times call for appointment

This line of contemporary sportswear is a hybrid of traditional equestrian garb and dancewear. It is designed, cut, sewn and shipped from Santa Barbara.

The Galop Fou label features coordinated leggings, tank tops, T-shirts and stirrup pants fashioned from high-grade cotton Lycra. Many garments feature Ultrasuede accents. Available in classic black and colors, the line is sized for women, children and toddlers. First quality merchandise is 30 percent below retail, seconds and discontinued styles and colors priced below cost.

Fiesta Hat Company Outlet

5045 Sixth Street
Carpinteria
684-7788
weekends only 10-5

Put a hat on your head and make a fashion statement—and smart move. With the hole in the ozone layer getting bigger all the time, it only makes good sense to wear a hat whenever you're outdoors. Fiesta Hat Company is one place to buy a hat with good looks at a great price. There's a wide selection of hats of all types—Panama hats (actually made in Equador)—baseball caps, cowboy hats, lifeguard, golf and children's hats, straws and felts for men and women, many of them made in the factory behind the hole-in-the-wall outlet store. You'll find first-quality overruns, discontinued styles, and the like, along with seconds of varying quality, all at seconds prices. All sales are final; cash only.

Firenze Factory Outlet

419 State Street
965-5723
Monday-Saturday 10-5:30; Sunday 12-5:30

The Firenze and M. Julian label suede and leather sportswear found in this snazzy shop is carried in department stores, boutiques and specialty catalogs across the country. The selection here includes seconds, overruns, seasonal merchandise and samples. Stock up at twice-yearly, half-price blowout sales (spring and fall).

Manufacturer's Sports Outlet

1134 Chapala Street
965-6652
Monday-Saturday 10-6; Sunday 12-5

Headquartered in San Luis Obispo, Manufacturer's Sports Outlet carries a great selection of gear for anyone whose idea of a workout is more physically demanding than a marathon shopping session. Runners, cyclists and swimmers are among the regular clientele.

Find first-quality Hind running shorts, tights, bathing suits and swimming trunks here, along with seconds, factory blemishes and close-outs—some at less than half-price.

Peaches & Cream

2003 State Street
682-6632
Monday-Saturday 10-6; Sunday 11-5

Peaches & Cream is a no-frills outlet shop open seasonally (spring and summer), specializing in women's and junior casual wear. All items in the Thin Air collection—loose-fitting rayon dresses, blouses, shorts and skirts—sell here for half regular retail price. Look also for Blue Pacific bathing suits, and bikinis, mini-dresses and playwear tagged with tiny prices.

Romika Factory Outlet

1 North Salsipuedes Street, #102
963-5971
Monday-Friday 9-4; first Saturday of each month 9-3

The fancy cars parked outside the Romika Factory Outlet are a tip-off to the quality of shoes shipped from this warehouse, the only U.S. distributor of these German shoes. Romikas feature long-wearing molded soles and are available here in men's women's and children's sizes at discounts from 30 to 50 percent. The selection includes close-outs, samples, cosmetic defects and overstock of first-quality footwear.

The Territory Ahead

27 East Mason Street
963-7633
Monday-Saturday 10-5:30; Sunday 11-5

Smartly styled men's clothing "American in spirit designed with a European flair." The outlet shop is an extension of the mail-order catalogue by the same name. Half the items on display are featured in the current catalog and sold here at full price, the other half are discontinued or last season's styles and colors. Some deals on pricey, classy clothes. A few items are sized and styled for women; many of the men's shirts and sweaters are suitable for women to wear.

Real Cheap Sports

36 West Santa Clara Street
Ventura (a bit of a schlepp, but worth it)
648-3803
Monday, Tuesday, Saturday 10-6; Wednesday, Thursday, Friday 10-8;
Sunday 11-5

Located just blocks from the international headquarters of Patagonia, the famed manufacturer of quality outdoor wear. The shop features close-outs, overruns, seconds and off-season gear, all at substantially below retail price (at least 30 percent). Ever-popular polar fleece garments at great prices, almost always a good selection of men's and women's pants, shorts and shirts. Look for first-quality "special make-ups" clothing created of leftover fabrics and trims available at outlet price. They also carry kayaks, sleeping boots and, occasionally, some odds and ends, such as backpacks and boots. A must stop for the outdoors person in the family (or those who just want to look like it).

Specialty Equipment

Magellan's Catalog Outlet Store
925 Punta Gorda Street
568-5400
Monday-Saturday 9-5:30
If you can't quite seem to get the knack of what to pack, this shop is just for you. Magellan's, a catalog order company headquartered in Santa Barbara claims, "If it makes travel more comfortable, safer, more convenient, and more enriching, we have it!"

The showroom contains many items at full current catalog price, along with a selection of discontinued and test market items ranging from 20 to 50 percent off catalog price. You'll find everything from basic accessories—travel alarm clocks and phrasebooks—to the exotic—multi-time zone watches and water purifying kits.

The shop's located on an unfamiliar street; it may test your navigational skills just a bit. Hint: it's close to the Red Lion Inn, just around the corner from Tri-County Produce, off Milpas Street. If you're a tourist longing to become a traveler, look for Magellan's to help you out.

Powell Peralta's Factory Outlet
30 South La Patera Lane
Goleta
964-1330, ext. 200
Monday-Tuesday 10-5; Wednesday-Friday 10-6; weekends 11-6
Located adjacent to the skateboard manufacturer's indoor skatepark is the showroom/factory outlet where skateboard fanatics can shop to their heart's content. Good selection of the company's skateboard decks, wheels, clothing and accessories. In this fast-moving sport products have a short shelf-life; lots of bargains in seconds and discontinued products at 30 to 50 percent off retail price.

Occasional blowout factory outlet sales are well advertised.

House and Garden

Angel Art Studio Outlet
9 West Ortega Street
962-5911
Tuesday-Saturday 11-6; Sunday 12-5
If your taste in decorating runs to the ethereal, check out the guardian angels, cherubs, seraphim and other plaster-cast figures carried at Angel Art. The designs are cast in historic molds derived from Baroque, Victorian and neo-Classical antique pieces—vases, columns, gravestones and the like. The line is carried at gift, interior furnishing and other specialty shops nationwide; buy first-quality merchandise here and just above wholesale price. You'll also find a line of T-shirts, gift wrap, stationery, picture frames, and even bath soaps, all featuring angel motifs.

Arte D'Italia
109 South Quarantina Street
564-7655
Monday-Friday 9:30-12:30; weekends by appointment only
Arte D'Italia is the sole distributor of the Parrucca collection of handmade ceramic ware imported from Palermo, Sicily. The one-of-a-kind Mediterranean folk art designs include pizza makers, grape stompers and orange pickers, along with whimsical fish, birds and dancers. The brightly colored motifs adorn platters, plates, serving dishes, vases and the like.

First-quality items, seen in gift and gourmet shops nationwide, sell here for 35 percent (or more) below retail; seconds sell for 20 percent below wholesale price.

Isabel Bloom of Santa Barbara
216 East Gutierrez Street
962-0904
Monday-Saturday 9-5; sometimes open on Sundays (call ahead)
Watch artisans create hand-crafted cement garden sculpture at Isabel Bloom. First-quality items range from whimsical California

critters—quail, pelicans and sea lions—to cheerful cherubs and elaborate recirculating fountains. Items for sale are five to ten percent below retail.

Santa Barbara Ceramic Design Studio Outlet

428 East Haley Street
966-3883
Monday-Saturday 9-6; Sunday 11-5

The hand-painted, nature-oriented ceramic designs created at Santa Barbara Ceramic Design are featured on an array of giftware and home accessories. The address plaques, clocks, picture frames, sundials and the like are sold in a number of department stores and nationally distributed catalogs.

Items sold as seconds may contain flaws such as an extra splash of paint or an off color, or they may be discontinued styles of prototypes. Also carried here is a selection of first-quality craft items, jewelry, rugs, glassware and the like at half-off the original price.

Jewelry

Iris Arc Crystal

114 East Haley Street

963-3661

open twice a year only

Let's make this crystal-clear: Iris Arc sells direct to the public only twice a year. Parking lot sales are held on the first Saturday in May and the first Saturday in December. The sale dates are perfect times to pick up gift items—paperweights, figurines, prisms, jewelry and more—all made of crystal. Many of the items offered for sale are retired designs or overruns, some are defective or slightly blemished. You've seen these lovely works of art, great-looking, sparkling crystal earrings, bracelets, pins, and even tie-clips in pricey gift shops and department stores; here's the place to buy them at huge discounts. During the parking lot sales, most items are priced at 70 to 90 percent off retail price.

Food

Let's face it, no matter what the cost, you gotta eat. So you might as well enjoy it, buy quality at the best price you can. You have two basic choices: fix it yourself or visit a restaurant and pay someone else to shop for and fix it for you.

If you're going to cook, it only makes sense to buy the freshest, tastiest ingredients to whip up simple, healthy meals. And if you're going to eat at a restaurant, it makes sense to get the best value for the tab. Sure, there's the occasional splurge when practicality goes right out the window, but the following offer suggestions about getting the most for your meals day after day. Consider the possibilities—a loaf of bread, a healthy salad, a little fresh fruit, a warm sunset, a soft breeze. . . .

Produce

Certified Farmer's Market

Locations and times (hours may vary with the season):
- Santa Barbara: Tuesday (early evening) 500 block of State Street; Saturday (8:30 to noon) corner of Cota and Santa Barbara streets
- Carpinteria: Tuesday (early evening), 800 Linden Avenue
- Goleta: Thursday (3-6:30), Calle Real Shopping Center

Buy seasonal produce direct from the grower. It's a lot more fun to check out the scene, taste samples, enjoy the party atmosphere as parking lots and city streets are transformed into colorful food bazaars. Lots of healthy, some organic produce, colorful flowers and fresh seafood—everything for a wonderful meal except bread and wine. Call 962-5354.

Farm Stands

There's an amazing island of green located in Goleta, where delicious produce has been grown and sold for decades. These colorful farm stands are a throwback to simpler times; patronizing them is a way to lend your support in a very tangible way to farmers who bring the bounty of the earth right out of their fields and direct to you.

I like buying produce where I can see the fields where it was grown, freshly picked and warm from the sun.

Fairview Gardens Farms

598 North Fairview Avenue
Goleta
967-7369 (messages only)
Friday-Wednesday, 10-6; closed November-March

Take your pick of fresh produce, eggs, tasty organic breads, fresh or dried flowers, and delicious peach butter—almost everything grown or gathered in the fields right behind the retail stand.

More than a produce stand, actually, this twelve-acre organic farm is a bit of rural America located in the heart of an urban environment. Michael Ableman, who has farmed this land for a decade, advocates community supported agriculture—simply put, before the growing season begins, consumers have the opportunity to purchase shares of the farm's budget; they then are entitled to their share of the harvest. This arrangement allows the farmer to use needed capital, and the shareholders get a healthy, fresh supply of food throughout the growing season. It's win-win all the way around.

For the 1993 season, seventy families signed on to Ableman's plan; you can participate in this innovative community project by purchasing your own share next year, or by purchasing produce at the stand. Be sure to get a punch card; when it's full ($50 worth), you get $4 off the next purchase.

Goleta Valley Farms

Hollister and Highway 217

Goleta

Monday-Saturday 9-6; Sunday 7:30-6; open all year

Located just around the corner from the airport, the green fields that support this stand are especially visible from a plane descending for a landing. Sweet strawberries, crisp corn and seedless watermelons are among the crops grown here and sold from this tiny stand.

Happy Harry's Produce

corner of Patterson & Hollister

Goleta

964-0400

8-6 every day (may close earlier on Sunday); open seasonally from the end of
  January through the end of October

This is a no-frills stand situated on a busy corner with good parking. It features locally grown produce, cut flowers and colorful live plants in full bloom. In early spring, the fuchsias are spectacular, as are the mini roses. One specialty is a great selection of Armstrong olives at very good prices.

Lane Farms "The Greenstand"

308 Walnut Lane (at Walnut and Hollister)
Goleta
964-3773
Monday-Saturday 9-6; Sunday 10-4; usually open February-November,
    but may stay open all year

The Lane family has operated The Greenstand since 1939, but they've been farming this land since the 1800s. Historic photographs, farm implements, license plates and framed newspaper articles adorn the walls, and are part of the charm of this produce stand. Toward the end of summer, this stand is known especially for its sweet corn, and in the fall its pumpkin patch is a wonder to behold.

A few baked goods, including Mark Olivier bread, eggs, and flowers are for sale along with the produce. There's a community bulletin board at the entrance of the stand, a nice touch.

Risley Produce

4950 Hollister Avenue
Goleta
683-5805
open every day 8:30-6 (open year-round)

"We're 100 percent organic," states farmer Peter Risley. "I'm fanatic about it." Much of the produce for sale here is grown on the five-acre farm located just behind the produce stand. A wide variety of organic produce, from arugula to zucchini, along with a few packaged goods and juices, herbs and sprouts comprise the selection here. The prices are good, the service excellent, and Risley's philosophy gives you something to think about when the strawberries are just a sweet memory. Munching fresh mulberries straight from the tree, he gestures toward his bustling market, "We farm to make a beautiful thing for people, to make people happier. This is food for the stomach and food for the soul."

Produce Markets

Mesa Produce
1905 Cliff Drive
962-1645
10-7 daily
Improbably located at a gas station situated on a busy corner of the Mesa, Mesa Produce almost always has the best selection of juicy, red and delicious tomatoes to be found. The atmosphere is breezy and friendly: signs offer help picking out melons, remind seniors (over 60) of their 10 percent dicount, and toddlers love to push the kid-sized grocery carts around.

Tri-County Produce Company
335 South Milpas Street
965-4558
Monday-Saturday 9-6:30; Sunday 9-6
The motto of this popular store is "If it's any fresher it's still in the fields." Believe it; the place looks like a farm stand that grew up— a great selection of every type of seasonal fresh produce plus bread, bulk dried fruit, cereals, trail mix, pastas, a dairy case, an extensive selection of wine, even packaged sandwiches. This is a convenient stop if you're planning a spur-of-the-moment picnic at the beach. (Remember Dan Quayle? Even he stopped here during a campaign swing through Santa Barbara.)

Bakeries

What could be better than a loaf of bread, freshly baked? It's one of life's simplest pleasures. While Angelenos swear that Il Fornaio bakes the only bread to die for (it's trucked in daily to Lazy Acres Market on the Mesa), locals have long enjoyed delicious fresh bread baked here in town. And in recent months, Santa Barbara has welcomed a couple of new bakeries (D'Angelo and Santa Barbara Bread Company) that rival even L.A.'s best. (Note: Not listed below, but also a wonderful baker is wholesale-only Marc Olivier; you can buy French loaves and baguettes in many local markets, including Tri-County Produce.)

D'Angelo

24 Parker Way
962-5466
Daily 7 a.m. to 2 p.m.
Those in the know show up at 6 o'clock looking for freshly baked. This is, quite simply, among the best bread I've ever tasted; baked in a stone-lined French oven, it's chewy, heavy, crusty and delicious. The bakers make bread the old-fashioned way—as in before the use of commercial yeast. They use wild yeast starters *(levain)* gleaned from the skins of Santa Ynez Valley grapes. Any left-over loaves are given to a local food bank.

Santa Barbara Bread Company

318 Milpas Street
568-0506
Monday-Saturday 7-5
The advertising campaign is inspired ("One Cannot Live on Bread Alone—We presume you have a little wine and cheese on hand"), and so is the bread. There are some fifteen fresh choices daily, including whole-wheat walnut, sun-dried tomato, fig and anise, and a dozen others. Limited seating available for breakfast, lunch and snacktime.

Our Daily Bread Bakery & Cafe

831 Santa Barbara Street
966-3894
Monday-Friday 7-5:30; Saturday 8-4

The tasty baguettes and large loaves of French bread, distinctively wrapped in their red-and-white paper bags, are available at markets throughout the Santa Barbara area. Other whole-grain and organic breads are sold here, and may be consumed on the premises or taken to go.

A Dining Deal

Discovery Dining

P.O. Box 5001
Santa Maria, CA 93456-9930
1-800-826-DINE

The type of coupon booklet offered by Discovery Dining is available in many communities across the nation. People who enjoy dining out and trying new restaurants may find the club membership a worthwhile investment. The membership fee (less than $30) entitles the purchaser to two-for-one dinners at a variety of popular restaurants and entertainment venues throughout the Central Coast. Most coupons are valid only on weekdays, and some restricted hours; the secret to getting your money's worth out of these booklets is to use them!

Coffeehouses

There is so much gourmet coffee in this town that even the down-town McDonald's serves cappuccino and espresso. Indulge at the Golden Arches if you must, but there are plenty of other alternatives from which to choose. Coffeehouses are the meeting places of the '90s, the hip spots to get a legal buzz from caffeine-loaded coffee concoctions, anytime day or night.

Cafe Siena
1101 State Street
963-7344
Monday-Thursday 7 a.m. to 11 p.m.; Friday 7 a.m. to midnight;
    Saturday 8 a.m to midnight; Sunday 8-11
Where else would you find a coffeehouse with a lava lamp?

Newly reopened following a fire that destroyed the old location a couple of years ago, this Siena is more sophisticated and offers a more extensive menu than before.

Enjoy the warm wood, Italian stone floor and faux finish on the walls of this one-time yogurt parlor turned-meeting place.

Coffee Cat
3615 State Street
569-8868
Monday-Friday 6-11:30 p.m.; Saturday and Sunday 7-11:30 p.m.
The coffeehouse goes post-industrial slick and clean with black matte and chrome, clean and spare interior. Pick up a "Coffee Cash" card for discounts on future visits. Special attractions include free coffee drink if you visit on the day of your name (i.e., Thurday Emily, Friday John, etc.; changes every week), videos screened 'round the clock, and a different movie every night.

Elsie's

117 West De La Guerra Street

963-4503

Daily 8 a.m.-midnight

The newest kid on the block, Elsie's opened Memorial Day weekend, 1993. Hidden away behind Paseo Nuevo, Elsie's has the atmosphere of a neighborhood coffeehouse. Its homey decor is reminiscent of the '50s, with Fiestaware and more kitchenettes than you've seen in several decades. This place is definitely interesting; there aren't many places where you can find a display of Charles and Diana memorabilia, an eighteenth-century stained glass window, and Pop-Tarts on the menu.

Espresso Roma

728 State Street

962-4721

Monday-Thursday 7 a.m. to 10 p.m.; Friday, 7 a.m. to 12:30 p.m.;
    Saturday 7:30 a.m to 12:30 a.m.; Sunday 8 a.m. to 11:30 p.m.

Espresso Roma is what a coffeehouse is all about: great coffee, interesting characters, cutting-edge art, and an atmosphere that has a bit of an edge to it. From professional people in the morning to creative types to Generation X, it's always an intriguing mix. Great place to hang out, but you wouldn't want to take your mom here when she's in town for a visit (unless she's totally hip).

The Green Dragon Art-Cafe

22 West Mission Street

687-1902

Daily 7 a.m. to midnight

The most mellow place in town; the Green Dragon features not only organic espresso, but delicious baked goods, sandwiches and daily specials.

The building, on the site of the one-time silent-film-era Flying A Studio, once housed a church. It seems to be filled with a certain spiritual presence, sometimes felt on quiet mornings, sometimes when the entertainment really touches your heart. Art exhibited on the walls, poetry readings, musical performances and drumming sessions from time to time. Write or draw your message for the masses on the roll of newsprint at the front entrance. A great place to go if you're very centered—or want to be.

Hestia House /Moore Coffee
1014 State Street
963-8060
Monday-Friday 6:30-11:00; Saturday 9 a.m. to midnight;
   Sunday 9 a.m. to 10 p.m.
The white walls and white tile floor are always clean and shiny, a little too clean for my taste in coffeehouses, and they allow smoking in the front section only, which is fine, except you have to walk through the haze to order a drink. Those objections aside, the place serves excellent coffee roasted on the premises, and is probably the only java joint around with a claw-footed bathtub-turned-planter on site. Specials include a Coffee Card for ten drinks at 30 percent off; $1 off on a pound of coffee of the day; one-third off espresso drink refills and one-third off with your own mug.

Hot Spots
36 State Street
963-4233
Daily 6 a.m. to midnight
Located just a half-block from Stearns Wharf, this espresso bar is also an information center for visitors. Sip a cappuccino and nibble a pastry while you examine pamphlets, maps and guidebooks, and plan your day's activities. Entertainment on weekends.

Pierre LaFond
(several locations throughout Santa Barbara and in Montecito)
Locals carry their royal blue Pierre LaFond insulated mugs wherever they go; it's a smart way to save resources and money. A mug full costs only 55 cents—what a deal. The coffee buyers' club deal allows members to get a free pound when you've bought a dozen. Great assortment of fresh pastries and delicious sandwiches, salads and main dishes for lunch.

Santa Barbara Roasting Company

321 Motor Way
962-0320
Daily 7 a.m.-midnight

This former hole-in-the-wall just keeps getting bigger and better, attracting an ever-growing following of bikies and beautiful people. Exquisite wooden bar and hand-painted murals contrast nicely with the corrugated ceiling, cement floor and parking lot ambience just outside the roll-up doors. Great coffee, too, roasted on the premises.

A Few Dozen Cheap Eats—
With a Little Help From My Friends

Here are some suggestions for cheap eats by longtime tourist-trap disdaining Santa Barbara residents.

Cheri Rae

"With all this shopping who has time to eat?
I need real food fast (as opposed to fast food)."

Tutti's Bakery
129 East Anapamu Street
962-2089
Daily 7 a.m. to 10 p.m.
Order something to go—a muffin and coffee, a sandwich and a salad, or a massive calzone (you have to share it)—and take it to the Courthouse Sunken Garden across the street for superb al fresco dining. Or eat in and enjoy a pasta dinner and the convivial trattoria-style ambience. (Don't miss the piped-in Italian lessons in the restrooms). Good place for breakfast.

Cafe Bianco
11 West Victoria Street
965-1977
Monday-Friday 7-6; Saturday 8-6
The whole-wheat pesto rolls are a crunchy, spicy treat and filling enough for lunch. Try the personal pizzas, scones and more elaborate dessert treats if you can afford the calories. Seating outside and on the upstairs terrace.

Earthling Cafe

1137 State Street

564-6096

Monday-Thursday 8 a.m. to 10:45; Friday 8 a.m. to 11:45;
    Saturday 9 a.m. to 11:45; Sunday 9 a.m. to 10:45

Try to figure out who's among the literary elite pictured on the mural-in-progess by local author/artist Barnaby Conrad. Meanwhile, sip a chardonnay and graze a salad, enjoy people-watching, catch snippets of conversation of literate shoppers, and devour the latest page-turner by your favorite author. Healthy light fare, quick service, and comfortable ambience. Take 20 percent off all espresso drinks during "Cappy Hour," 5:30 to 7:30 every evening (order decaf so you can sleep).

Stanton's Gourmet Pizza

411 State Street

965-1983

Sunday-Thursday 11:30-10:00; Friday and Saturday 11:30-11:00

A slice of pesto and eggplant pizza (or anything else that's already made and ready to serve) and something to drink for a low-cost (if not low-cal) lunch or dinner-right-before-a-movie-and-we-don't-have-much-time.

Espressway Cafe

310 Chapala Street

966-5636

Monday-Friday 11-3, 5-11 p.m.; Weekends 7-3, 5-11

Located right next to the freeway at the end of Chapala Street, is the aptly named Espressway Cafe (but because of impending seismic work, is moving to another location sometime soon). Open for breakfast and lunch, and later for dinner, the fare includes healthy salads and pastas, innovative sandwiches and soups, omelets and more. One room offers coffee shop decor, while the other has dressed up tables with linen cloths; limited outdoor seating.

Taqueria Cuca

315 Meigs Road

966-5951

9 a.m to 10 p.m.

Order huge carne asada super burrito when you haven't eaten for a few days (or share it with a friend). It's stuffed with beans, rice, tasty beef and lots of delicious flavors. The aguas frescas are refreshing (especially strawberry). Quick, friendly service and colorful decor.

Italian Grocery

415 De La Guerra Street

966-6041

Monday-Saturday, 8-6; Sunday 9-2

My Sicilian grandparents used to take me with them when they shopped in grocery stores like this one. I still love the pungent smells, the colorful imported foods lining the shelves. This place reminds me of my early years, with its pungent aromas, the colorful imported foods lining the shelves. The huge special submarine sandwich, the super deluxe (share it with a friend), comes close to the ones Mama used to make.

The Nugget

2318 Lillie Avenue

Summerland

969-6135

Monday-Friday 11-9 or 10; Saturday 11-10; Sunday 8:30 a.m. to 10 p.m.

President-elect Clinton and his entourage ate here during their Thanksgiving West Coast visit; photos and autographs adorn the walls, along with a saxophone designated for Bill to play whenever he's in town. Whatever your politics, the place is known for its down-home ambience, burgers and beer. It's a colorful Summerland hang-out for locals and a favorite stop for travelers from L.A.

Need a little exercise after your meal? Head across the railroad tracks to Lookout County Park and walk off some of those calories.

John McKinney

*(Nature writer with a stomach of steel, he swears that
breakfast is the only important meal of the day and
that a little swill never hurt anybody)*

"If you hunger for more than a coffee 'n' roll Euro-breakfast,
I have three favorites. All three serve lunch, too—
mostly burgers and sandwiches—but excel at breakfast."

Esau's Coffee Shop

403 State Street
965-4416
Monday-Friday, 6 a.m. to 2 p.m.; Sat-Sun, 7 a.m.- 2 p.m.

Ever since Tom Esau set up his griddle at this location, Esau's has been a popular breakfast spot. The eatery serves a big breakfast—grits, scrambled combos, and lots of potatoes—but is especially known for its pancakes, the best in town: buttermilk, wheat germ, blueberry and banana cakes served in mini and Mickey Mouse stacks for light eaters, short and full stacks for hearty and the heartiest of appetites.

For the best deals, consult the blackboard for daily specials or, Monday through Thursday, try the 2-2-2 (two pancakes, two eggs, two strips of bacon) for about three bucks. This is a very popular place on weekends; it's not uncommon to see a line snaking out the door down State Street. Esau's popularity is easy to see, particularly now that they've upgraded their coffee from what was among the worst swill in Santa Barbara to at least an acceptable level and now offer Caribbean coffee and cappuccino, no less.

Judge For Yourself Cafe

1218 Santa Barbara Street
966-9000
Daily 7 a.m. to 2 p.m.

This locals-only cafe is conveniently located near the Courthouse. As its name suggests, it draws cops and lawyers as well as downtown workers looking for a hearty breakfast to start the day. The terribly punny menu features dozens of items on the Egg-Genda.

Exhibit A is two pancakes, two eggs, two strips of bacon; Exhibit B is a potato skins concoction that must be seen to be believed. Check the daily chalkboard specials. Light-to-moderate eaters might want to split one of the Judge's rather large omelets.

Mesa Cafe

1972 Cliff Drive
966-5303
Monday-Saturday 6 a.m. to 10 p.m.; Sunday 6 a.m. to 9 a.m.

The Mesa Cafe draws fishermen, city college students, harbor folks, guys and gals who work for a living. It's remained undiscovered by tourists, but is popular with locals, who banter with the friendliest waitresses in town.

The daily special—scrambled eggs with various vegetables and cheeses, and accompanied by potatoes or fruit and toast or muffin—will fill you up and only set you back about three bucks. Omelets, pancakes and other breakfast items are also reasonably priced. Check the chalkboard for daily specials. Al fresco dining is available in an outdoor seating area out front.

Beyond Breakfast...

Castagnola Brothers Fish Gallery

205 Santa Barbara Street
962-8053
Daily 11-9

I like the fish and chips at this order-at-the-counter eatery. Eat inside or outside on the patio; better yet, douse your meal with vinegar or catsup and walk two blocks to the beach.

Joe's Cafe

536 State Street
966-4638
Monday-Saturday 11-11; Sunday 4-10

A Santa Barbara institution, that's Joe's—where an average American cuisine added to so-so atmosphere and Santa Barbara's best salsa (try it on buttered bread!) somehow total up to a very pleasant dining experience. Try to get a booth on the bar side of Joe's (so you can Santa Barbara people-watch), put your elbows on the glassed-over, red-checkered tablecloth, and order something meaty: the must-be-tried-to-be-believed beefy Omaha Sandwich or Joe's special New York steak. The open-faced turkey sandwich is pretty good, too.

La Tolteca
614 East Haley Street
963-0847
7 a.m. to 8 p.m.
Tacos, tostadas, burritos and enchiladas are made fresh to order, meaning that although the walk-up counter suggests fast food, the food is not quickly prepared; that's okay, because it gives you a few minutes to stroll next door and check out the tortilla factory. Tortilla technology looks kinda complex, huh? Sit at one of few tables inside, or outside on the sidewalk.

Paradise Cafe
702 Anacapa Street
962-4416
Monday-Saturday 11-11; Sunday 8:30 a.m. to 11 p.m.
The price of paradise can be dear if you order one of their fresh fish specials at dinnertime, but some entrées are budget. And the cafe, with its al fresco dining, California cuisine with a Santa Barbara spin and its overall ambiance adds up to a good deal, when you factor in surroundings. Paradise serves up an awesome Cobb salad and a pretty good Greek salad. The Calamari sandwich is a Greco-American delight. And I just happen to think the Paradise Burger is best grilled cow in town.

Woody's BBQ
229 West Montecito Street
963-9326
Monday-Saturday 11-11; Sunday 11-10
No place for faint-hearted vegetarians, Woody's serves up the best barbecue in town. Best bets are the slabs of beef and pork ribs,

slathered in sauce, and served with cole slaw, beans, fries and bread. The feeling of eating like a pig is accentuated by the restaurant's barn-like interior decorating, complete with farm implements hanging on the wall. Beer is served in Mason jars and they're generous with napkins.

Pino's Italian Pizzeria

5863 Hollister Avenue
Goleta
967-1933
Monday-Friday 11-1:30, 5-9:30; Saturday-Sunday 11-1:30, 5-10
Pino's makes one of the best pizzas in town, but a better reason to go is the made-from-scratch pasta dishes. From the most basic spaghetti and meatballs or spaghetti olio to the homemade ravioli and terrific seafood combo, Pino does pasta right—and entertains customers (the whole family is welcome) with Italian songs and opera. Pino's prices are not bargain basement, but a good deal considering everything's made fresh, and considering the alternative—some of the worst Italian restaurants on the planet are located in downtown Santa Barbara, and some very good but very pricey trattorias are in Montecito.

Sojourner Coffeehouse

134 East Canon Perdido Street
965-7922
Monday-Saturday 11-11; Sunday 5 p.m. to 10 p.m.
Folks, it just doesn't get any more mellow than flashback-to-the-'60s "Soj." The Birkenstock brigade, university professors, and vegetarians of every stripe enjoy tostadas, rice-and-vegetable plates, stuffed baked potatoes. Good deals are the Soj Burger and the Low-Rent Special—a bowl of soup, bread, and salad. If you want a budget meal at the Soj, stay away from the pricier daily chalkboard specials and the adult beverages. If you're dining alone, sit down at the counter and mix and mingle with the locals.

Steve Hoegerman

*(Native Santa Barbaran, creator of the French Festival,
bon vivant, entrepeneur, gourmet, gourmand, advertising whiz)*

Fennel
1812 Cliff Drive
962-0337
Monday-Friday 10-9; Saturday and Sunday 9-9; limited menu 3-5
Brigitte creates healthy, interesting veggie dishes gone gourmet, in a European country-atmosphere on the Mesa.

Jimmy's Oriental Gardens
126 East Canon Perdido
962-7582
Wednesday, Thursday, Sunday 5-10; Friday and Saturday 5-11
Chow mein comes complete with hot tea and a fortune cookie in the last remnant of Santa Barbara's Chinese district, improbably located directly across from the Presidio.

Main Squeeze
138 East Canon Perdido Street
966-5365
A bowl of soup (choice of two) and bread make a good rainy day lunch.

Moo Shi Factory
6530 Pardall Road
Isla Vista
968-9766
Daily 11:30-10
Great Chinese combos.

Your Place

22-A North Milpas Street
966-5151
Tuesday-Thursday 11-10; Friday and Saturday 11-11; Sunday 11-10
I always get the curry noodles at Your Place, winner of the *Santa Barbara Independent*'s Living Legend award. Great lunch specials.

Zelo

630 State Street
966-5792
Tuesday night is Pasta Night; $6.95 for any pasta dish including a big salad. Also runs ads regularly "Dinner for Two, $15." This a good value.

Francess Lantz

(Children's book author, former restaurant reviewer for the
Santa Barbara Independent, *and a busy mom who hates to cook)*

Breakwater Restaurant
At the Harbor
965-1557
Daily 7 a.m. to 8:30 p.m. (or 9:00)
Friendly greasy-spoon fish restaurant with good fish and chips; frequented by local fishermen.

Caribbean Cuisine
5838 Hollister Avenue
Goleta
967-7265
Monday-Friday 11-2, 5-9; Saturday 5-whenever
Jamaican food, including killer jerk pork and chicken. Live reggae on the weekends.

Dutch Garden
4203 State Street
967-4911
Tuesday-Saturday 11-8
Good German food, especially reasonable at lunch, funky outdoor seating.

Flavor of India
3026 State Street
682-6561
Daily 5:30-10
All-you-can-eat lunch buffet is a real deal. A good introduction to the world of Indian cuisine.

La Super-Rica Taqueria

622 Milpas Street (at the corner of Alphonse Street, easier to find than the
    restaurant sign; park up the street, the lot is impossible)
963-4940
Sunday-Thursday 11-9:30; Friday-Saturday 11-10

Authentic Mexican tacos, handmade corn tortillas. Cheap unless
you get carried away and buy a dozen, which is easy to do. (This
restaurant is always cited by major foodies, including the vener-
able Julia Child, Ruth Reichl and Merrill Schindler.)

The Oak Pit

Highway 33 in Oak View, on the way to Ojai
649-9903
Tuesday-Thursday and Sunday 11-8:30; Friday-Saturday 11-9;

(Okay, I cheated, it's not in Santa Barbara, but it's worth the
drive). Real Texas barbecue in a country-and-western atmosphere.
The beef and pork sandwiches with cole slaw are your best bet.

Palazzio

1511 Coast Village Road
Montecito
969-8565
Monday-Friday 11:30-2:30, 5:30-10 (coffee and dessert 'til 11);
    Saturday-Sunday 11:30-11 (coffee and dessert 'til 12)

Good northern Italian food; doesn't seem all that cheap until you
discover the portions are monstrously huge.

Rose Cafe

424 East Haley Street
966-3773
Daily 7 a.m. to 9:30 p.m.

Real down-home Mexican cooking; my favorite dish is machaca
with cheese (eggs, shredded beef, green peppers and onions
scrambled together).

Santa Barbara Shellfish Company

End of Stearns Wharf

963-4415

Hours vary with the sun; Summer hours are Monday-Thursday 10-8;
Friday 10-8:30; Saturday-Sunday 10-9

Seafood salads, peel-'em-yourself shrimp, great view, but you have to fight off the seaguls.

Skandi Buffet

2911 De La Vina Street

682-3141

Monday-Friday 11-4 (lunch) 4-8:30 (dinner); Saturday 4-8:30;
Sunday 11:30-8

All you can eat Scandinavian food, cheaper than a trip to Solvang.

Food

Michael Zolkoski

*(Former-restaurateur-turned-gourmet-cook,
committed jogger who runs off extra calories every day,
bargain-hunter from way back.)*

Maikai

1279 Coast Village Road
Montecito
969-2190
Sunday-Thurs 11 a.m.-9:30 p.m.; Friday and Saturday 11 a.m.- 10 a.m.
Hawaiian burrito? Why not. Big portions, nothing over $5.50

Brophy Bros.

119 Harbor Way
966-4418
Sunday-Thursday, 11 a.m.-10 p.m.; Friday-Saturday 11 a.m.-11 p.m.
Order clam chowder or cioppino with salad and a tall drink. Grab
a seat the bar. Bring a friend and catch the local scene.

Sea Cove

801 Shoreline Drive
965-2917
Daily 8 a.m.-9 p.m.
Good food, not cheap, but unbeatable, almost-like-home. Great
live jazz nightly. A bargain for your buck.

Kashima

5746 Hollister
Goleta
683-8724
Monday-Friday 11:30 a.m.-2 p.m., 5-10 p.m.; Saturday 5-10 p.m.;
    closed Sunday
Where the local Japanese go to eat. Noodle-and-rice dishes,
$5-$6. Top quality.

Divine Decadence

When you want to indulge, throw caution to the wind and try these local specialties—for dessert, for celebration, for fun.

Santa Barbara Cheesecake

1915 De La Vina Street
687-3321
Tuesday-Saturday noon-5:30

This small family operation has been in business for thirteen years—with no advertising except word-of-mouth—and no less a food expert than Julia Child has recommended it! Owners Peter and Lois Clarke attribute their success to their insistence on quality ingredients: No artificial anything; everything made from scratch, including the crusts. Special orders for diabetics, those with allergies to wheat or nuts; seasonal specialties include pumpkin in the fall. A slice of plain cheesecake with raspberry sauce is the most popular (and least caloric) choice.

McConnell's Ice Cream

201 West Mission Street
569-2323
Daily 11 a.m. to midnight
and
1213 State Street
965-5400
Sunday-Thursday 11-11; Friday and Saturday 11 a.m. to midnight

McConnell's has been making its quality ice cream in Santa Barbara since 1963. Less than twenty years later, in 1981, *Time* magazine called McConnell's ice cream "the best ice cream in the world." Few ice cream lovers would disagree. McConnell's is very rich, at 22 percent butterfat; with no fillings or stabilizers it's the real thing. Amongst all this delicious temptation, they offer a fat- and sugar-free hot fudge topping—what, for a diet hot-fudge sundae?

Regular customers know when the staff is changing frozen yogurt flavors—they can buy a quart of yogurt for the price of a pint. And anyone can take advantage of the "Weight Watchers" special: buy a quart, get a pint free.

Robitaille's Fine Candies

900 Linden Avenue
Carpinteria
684-9340
Monday-Saturday 10-5; Sunday 10-2

Got a sweet tooth? Satisfy it with a visit to Robitaille's. The candy makers supplied the Official Mint of the Fiftieth Presidential Inauguration (Reagan's second), and aren't about to let anyone forget it. Republican politicos' photographs and memorabilia decorate the place (along with that of hockey pro and distant relative Luc Robitaille); but the reason to come here isn't the decor, it's the quality candy made right on the premises. Old-fashioned licorice whips and handmade fudge, almond bark and luscious caramels— not penny candy, but worth every cent.

Fun & Games

From daily bargain matinees to annual ethnic festivals, Santa Barbara offers something for everybody every season of the year. To have the most fun, use your imagination and pursue your own interests; here are some suggestions to help you get started.

Reel Deals

If word of these deals ever gets out, it'll be SRO at every venue from now on.

A Standing Ovation for Bargain Prices

Metropolitan Theatres, owner of every movie house in town (Fiesta 5, Paseo Nuevo, Metro, Riviera, Arlington, Fairview Twin, Plaza de Oro, Cinema Twin, Granada), has several ways to save the high price of a movie ticket. Bargain matinees (before 4:00), Monday through Friday, tickets are $5 for adults, $4 for seniors and $3.50 for children. Twi-light shows (4:00-6:00) everyday, all tickets are just $3.50. Call the Movie Hotline at 963-9503 for program information.

Twofers

The **Plaza de Oro Theatre**, located off the beaten path at 349 Hitchcock Way, usually screens double features for just $3.50. These are often films that were shown downtown for relatively short runs (some if you blinked you missed them), and screenings are often in the evenings only.

Remember the Vic?

The late, great **Victoria Theatre**, a movie house without a home, now screens the best in foreign and off-beat films at various locales throughout town, most regularly at the Bluebird Cafe, 1221 State Street (upstairs in Victoria Court).

Encore, Encore

The **Riviera Theatre**, a hidden gem located at 2044 Alameda Padre Serra on the Riviera, runs a Sunday Encore series of classic foreign and American films each Sunday morning at 11:00; tickets are just $4.00. For showtimes and dates call 965-3886.

Do-it-Yourself

There are video rental shops everywhere, but the only one for real cinema lovers is **Video Schmideo**, located downtown at 11 West

Victoria Street (in Victoria Court). The motto says it all: "It's the reel thing." Look for informational handouts, movies arranged by actor, director, country and other more colorful categories. They even have a playroom for kids. Take advantage of the Recession Wednesday special when movies rent for 2-for-1; 564-4999.

Be True to Your School

UCSB Arts & Lectures regularly screens standout films that you might have missed the first time around, or first-runs that may not make it to general release. Some are free, others cost $3-5, sometimes the films are presented in a series with a special price. Whatever the deal, call 893-3535 for current information, and ask to receive the monthly calendar.

We are All Earthlings

Earthling Bookshop's film club screens classic films every Tuesday night at 7:00, often introduced by an actor, director or producer associated with the film. On Wednesdays, local photographers present travel slide shows at 7:15. Both events are free of charge.

Freebies

The best things in life are free, especially in Santa Barbara. Try these:

• Walks on the beach: Butterfly Beach in Montecito; Stearns Wharf to the Breakwater along the shore; Arroyo Burro Beach (locals call it Hendry's—the "d" is silent); East Beach from Stearns Wharf to the volleyball courts

• Watch the sunset from Franceschi Park and take in breathtaking views of the entire city, from the Riviera to the ocean.

• Tour the famed County Courthouse (inside and out), then take the elevator to the top floor to enjoy the expansive view from the tower. Compare your thoughts about compass points with the ones on the roof, and speculate about the state of mind of the city engineer (popular myth is that he was drunk or completely incompetent) who laid out Santa Barbara's street system oriented to nothing in particular.

• Stroll through the Mission Rose Garden and read every identifying plaque; see how many you can remember next trip.

• Examine the art showing at the Faulkner Gallery in the Library.

• Picnic under and ponder the Chromatic Gate, the steel-edged rainbow sculpture on Cabrillo Boulevard.

• Stroll through the remarkably artistic Santa Barbara Cemetery, located at the east end of Cabrillo Boulevard where it meets Channel Drive. It features architecture by George Washington Smith, frescoes by Alfredo Ramos Martinez, headstones of the rich and famous (even in eternal repose they enjoy the best coastal property), and some of the best mountain and coastal vistas in town.

• Enjoy sand, surf and most of all, beach volleyball at East Beach. Even Bill "Spike" Clinton gets in a few digs here on his trips to the coast.

• Every Sunday take in the Arts and Crafts Show that stretches along Cabrillo Boulevard from Stearns Wharf halfway to Montecito. Some art, lots of crafts some you decide.

• Museum of Art Free on Thursday; Museum of Natural History Free on Wednesday (plan accordingly)

• Downtown people-watching, from the amphitheater at Paseo Nuevo to the fireplace at the Earthling, the beach from one end to the other, there's no better place than Santa Barbara to enjoy the art of watching the world go by.

Attractions

For a city its size, Santa Barbara has an astonishing number of museums and other cultural attractions. Most offer memberships which are an excellent value, especially if you're a frequent patron.

Channing Peake Gallery
105 East Anapamu Street
568-3432
Monday-Friday 8:30-5
Located at County Administration Building; exhibits work of the Santa Barbara County Arts Commission; affiliated with Art in Public Places program; free.

El Presidio de Santa Barbara State Historic Park
123 East Canon Perdido Street
965-0093
Daily 10:30-4:30
One of four Spanish military outposts established in California; ambitious plans to reconstruct the complex are underway by Santa Barbara Trust for Historic Preservation; free.

Fernald House and Trussell-Winchester Adobe
414 West Montecito Street
966-1601
Sunday 2-4
Trace Santa Barbara's changing architectural styles exemplified in these designated state historical landmarks: an adobe gone nautical and a true Victorian showpiece; free.

Karpeles Manuscript Library
21 West Anapamu Street
962-5322
Daily 10-4
Original documents and manuscripts on display; collection includes letters penned by Napoleon, Albert Einstein, George Washington, Abraham Lincoln and others; free.

Old Mission Santa Barbara

2201 Laguna Street
682-4713
Daily 9-5
The "Queen of the California Missions"; the grounds, exhibits, gardens and sanctuary provide insights into California's earliest beginnings; admission charge.

Old Spanish Days Carriage Museum

129 Castillo Street (in Pershing Park)
962-2353
Sunday 2-4
Largest collection of restored wheeled conveyances in the West: seventy-five coaches, wagons, carriages, carts, etc.; free.

Santa Barbara Botanic Garden

1212 Mission Canyon Drive
682-4726
Daily 9-sunset
Miles of trails through native plants; offers classes and special programs; daily docent tours; admission charge.

Santa Barbara Contemporary Arts Forum

563 Paseo Nuevo Mall
966-5373
Tuesday-Saturday 10-5
Gallery for the exhibition and performance of quality contemporary art; community outreach programs; free.

Santa Barbara County Courthouse

1100 Anacapa Street
962-6464
Daily 9-5
Not just a tourist attraction, the seat of county government; don't miss the Sunken Gardens, view from the tower, carved quotations, Chumash canoe, tile murals; daily tours; free.

Santa Barbara Museum of Art

1130 State Street
963-4364
Tuesday-Saturday 11-5 (Thursday 11-9); Sunday 12-5
Most extensive collection of art on the Central Coast; docent tours daily; admission charge (thanks to Cox Cable, free admission every Thursday and the first Sunday of the month).

Santa Barbara Historical Museum and Gledhill Library

136 East De La Guerra Street
966-1601
Tuesday-Saturday 10-5; Sunday 12-5
Early Santa Barbara/California collection on display; research library; historic adobes on the grounds; free.

Santa Barbara Museum of Natural History

2559 Puesta del Sol Road
682-4711
Monday-Saturday 9-5; Sunday and holidays 10-5
Dioramas and displays reveal human and natural history of the area; planetarium, observatory; admission charge (free Wed.).

Sea Center

211 Stearns Wharf
963-1067
Monday-Friday 11-7 (summer); 12-5 (non-summer); Weekends and holidays
    11-6; Touch Tank 12-4
Exhibits to educate about the area's marine environment; includes dioramas and models, high-tech displays; admission charge.

Santa Barbara Zoological Gardens

500 Niños Drive
962-5339
Daily 9-6 (summer); 10-5 (non-summer)
Natural settings house 500 critters; train, petting zoo and plenty of room for kids to run in playground and lovely hillsides; admission charge.

University Art Museum
UCSB
893-2951
Tuesday-Saturday 10-4; Sunday 1-5
Contemporary and historical art; lectures, panel discussions; tours.

Annual Events

A selective guide to the best and the brightest of Santa Barbara's unbelievable number of days set aside to celebrate something.

Santa Barbara International Film Festival
Each March, Santa Barbarans are in the dark—and happy about it. Two weeks of celebrities, premieres and screenings of U.S. and foreign films—a must for cinephiles.

Get more movies for your money when you purchase one of several special discount passes. Call 963-0023.

I Madonnari Italian Street Painting Festival
Every Memorial Day Weekend the parking lot of the Santa Barbara Mission becomes an art gallery. Practicing the ages-old art of street painting, a couple hundred local artists create striking tableaux, drawing with chalk right on the asphalt. The results are astonishingly beautiful, intriguing, and lots of fun to view. The event is free to the public; proceeds from concessions sales benefit the Childen's Creative Project. (Hint: The paintings remain until they wear away; viewing them with the weekend crowds is fun, but plan a return trip during the week to really appreciate the artwork.)

Solstice Parade
Celebrate the longest day of the year with most colorful parade in town. State Street comes alive each June on Solstice Saturday with whimsical costumes, energetic dancers and the beat of a thousand drums. This kickoff to summer shouldn't be missed. After the pa-

rade, picnic in Alameda Park, and later head over to the Courthouse for wondrous performances in the Sunken Garden.

Santa Barbara Writer's Conference

Each June, internationally known literati and wannabes gather at the Miramar Hotel for the Santa Barbara Writer's Conference for a week of intensive workshops and the opportunity to share their work, insights and interests. Among the speakers featured at previous conferences are Maya Angelou, James Michener, Amy Tan, and Tony Hillerman. Workshops and some special events are for conference attendees only, but lectures by notable speakers are open to the public throughout the week for just $6. Contact Santa Barbara Writers Conference, P.O. Box 304, Carpinteria, CA 93014

Semana Náutica (Marine Week)

A week-long celebration of sports, with events scheduled at parks and beaches all over town. From softball games to lawn bowls, weightlifting to ocean swimming events, it's the summertime (July) sports extravaganza that has attracted athletes and fans from all over the southland for the past half-century.

Old Spanish Days (Fiesta)

"Viva La Fiesta!" is the cry heard all over town when Fiesta fever hits each August. It's a celebration of Santa Barbara's Spanish heritage, and includes a weekday parade, food marketplaces and colorful performances at various locales.

Oak Park Cultural Festivals

(spring through fall)

Increase your cultural awareness without leaving home. Santa Barbara has become home to a multitude of wonderful festivals that celebrate diversity and reinforce the commonality between people. Each features the distinctive music and dance, food and drink, clothing and arts of the culture.

Enjoy the wooded ambiance of lovely Oak Park, and be sure to arrive hungry so you can sample delicious treats. Wear comfortable walking shoes, and dress for a warm day (don't forget the sunscreen); plan on a full day of outdoor dining and dancing with plenty of company. When the day gets in full swing, it's nearly impossible to cross the bridge over Mission Creek, but the crowd is part of the fun. Admission is free. Park a few blocks away in the residential area and walk to the festivities.

Dates change yearly; the 1993 calendar included the following:

Jewish Festival (May 2; call 968-1280)

Children's Festival (always the Saturday before Mother's Day; call 969-7235)

Irish Festival (June 5 & 6; call 969-0571)

French Festival (usually the weekend closest to Bastille Day; July 17 & 18; call 564-2525)

Greek Festival (usually the last weekend in July; July 31 & August 1; call 683-4492)

Italian Festival (August 28 & 29; call 687-7197)

Mexican Independence Festival (September 18 & 19; call 962-5500)

German Oktoberfest (October 2 & 3; call 962-2235)

Santa Barbara Jazz Festival

Celebrate Indian Summer with some cool tunes and hot licks at Leadbetter Beach. This mellow weekend event is held the first weekend of October, sponsored by the Sea Cove Restaurant.

FYI:
A few resources to help you find your own bargains

A Down-Home Philosophy

Buy Santa Barbara Alliance

This organization of local merchants has as mission statement: "To nurture the prosperity, growth, and survival of the greater Santa Barbara business community by encouraging the referral and purchasing of products and services from locally owned businesses."

The Buy Santa Barbara Alliance runs radio ads featuring the aw-shucks, folksy voice of Motel 6 pitchman Tom Bodette; members meet for lunch once a week and must be having some effect—you see their bumper stickers plastered on vehicles all over town. Contact the Buy Santa Barbara Alliance at P.O. Box 3310, Santa Barbara, CA 93130; 564-6140.

Media

The Santa Barbara Independent

The most comprehensive source of information about Santa Barbara's art and entertainment scene is *The Independent,* a free weekly tabloid widely available at newsstands, news racks and shops along State Street. Published every Thursday, the paper includes critical reviews, movie listings, nightclubs, lectures and meetings, along with features about political and social issues.

Each issue includes money-saving coupons, notices about upcoming sales and great classified ads. Bulletin Board ads (found on the last page of the paper) offer deals on everything from deep tissue massage to Japanese language courses; from flying lessons to a low-cost divorce.

The Santa Barbara News-Press

The *Santa Barbara News-Press,* owned by the New York Times Company, is California's longest continuously published newspaper. Friday editions include *Scene* magazine, with news and reviews about local entertainment, artists and events (many of the free). And every Tuesday, the *News-Press* runs The Classified Attic, a special section of classified ads for items priced at $75 or less. They may range from furniture to exercise equipment, wedding dresses to used bricks. It's fun to skim through, a good place to advertise the "bargains" accumulating in your garage or around your house.

KTMS Radio Mall

The station calls it "The Absolutely Amazing KTMS AM 1250 Radio Mall"; you can think of it as the Home Shopping Network of the air. Weekday afternoons from 12:15 to 2:00 p.m., and Saturdays from 1:00 to 2:00 p.m., on radio station KTMS (AM 1250) listen in for special offers and discounts on goods and services offered by local businesses. Save up to 50 percent (or more) by purchasing special certificates discounting restaurant meals, retail shops, personal services, automotive repairs, and a wide variety of household repairs and services. For big bargains and the convenience of shopping by phone, listen to the show, pick the special offer that interests you, and call the radio station at 899-2200 during the show's hours.

Shop 'til You Drop Without Going Broke

Unique shops where you can easily find out-of-the-ordinary small gifts (and items for yourself) with price tags to match:

Beads
622 State Street
966-1138
Monday-Saturday 10-6; Sunday 12-5
Use your imagination—and all sorts of beads—to make unique jewelry: earrings, necklaces, bracelets, pins and anything else you can come up with. There are samples everywhere to give you ideas. This place is a delight especially for creative teen-agers, their moms and grandmothers.

Brush and Needle
6 West Anapamu Street
564-8468
Monday-Saturday 10-5:30
Whenever I go on vacation I like to buy a stitchery project that reminds me of the place and time away (finding time to complete these projects is another matter entirely). The mother-and-daughter team of Loretta Minor and Donna Venzor run the type of place I'd want to find on vacation. It's a complete stitchery shop in town, carrying needlepoint, cross stitch and crewel work (they even stock a couple of chart designs of the Mission and the County Courthouse). A large selection of threads, handpainted needlepoint canvases and a special deal: when you complete a punch card (totalling $115 worth of purchases), you can take $20 off your next purchase.

Enlightened Sights
819 State Street
962-3008
Monday-Friday 10-9; Saturday 10-7; Sunday 10-6
A great selection of cards, ranging from sweetly charming to adults-only, one of the best newsstands in town, and lots of fun

stuff—mobiles, hand-crafted jewelry, gift wrap suitable for framing, refrigerator magnets (my favorite is the one of President Clinton and Vice-President Al Gore as beachboy hunks), and fragrant lotions and potions. Friendly atmosphere, and consistently interesting (and often thought-provoking) window displays.

Jordano's Kitchen Supply

614 Chapala Street
965-3031
Monday-Saturday 10-6; Sunday 12-5
Everything for the good cook; look for every utensil ever made. Colorful potholders; low-cost bistro glasses, spices and Santa Barbara specialty foods are the biggest bargains here. You could easily drop $10,000 here creating your dream kitchen, but for as little as $10 you could have a lot of fun picking out accessories.

Judith Geiger Gallery

10 West Figueroa Street
564-1881
Monday, Wednesday-Saturday 11-5; Tuesday and Sunday by chance
The colorful, whimsical art of well-known artist Judith Geiger is displayed in this tiny gallery. Choose from original hand-painted silks, or reproductions of her work on everything from T-shirts to coffee mugs, earrings and pins. Also look for wind-up toys guaranteed to delight the child within. Fun stuff.

Margo's Barbie

3204-C State Street
Tuesday-Saturday 12-5
687-5677
Got a little girl who loves Barbie? This is the place for her: postcards, clothes, jewelry, collectibles of all types, including ethnic Barbies—from Eskimo to Greek, Aussie to Italian; Flapper and Gibson Girl-Barbies, and even Army Barbie. Owner Margo Rana has been a collector since she was a child; she even has a life-sized Barbie mannequin that's sometimes on display.

Paradise Found

17 East Anapamu Street
564-3573
Monday-Saturday 10-6; Sunday 12-6
Everything for the New-Ager: A wide selection of tapes and CDs (try before you buy in a comfortable audio booth) books, jewelry, crystals, talismans, dreamcatchers and the like in the town's most tranquil environment.

Stampa Barbara

505 Paseo Nuevo
962-4077
Monday-Friday 10-9; Saturday 10-7; Sunday 11-6
You could easily get carried away and spend a fortune at the world's largest rubber stamp emporium, but you don't have to. Rubber stamps make great low-cost gifts (think names, hobbies, favorite characters and expressions, and so much more) for everyone on your list.

Zebra

22 West Mission Street
687-3767
Tuesday-Thursday and Sunday 10-8; Friday and Saturday 10-11 p.m.
If you're searching for "uncommon objects and creative clothing," Zebra is the shop for you. Treasures from around the world—and right here in Santa Barbara—including jewelry, musical instruments, children's clothing and toys, cards, and whimsical hand-crafted items.

Music, Music, Music

American Pie Records

600 North Milpas Street

965-2161

Monday-Saturday 10-6:30

The only record-only store in the Tri Counties specializes in classic rock 'n' roll on vinyl. Mention the words "CD" or "digitally remastered" and watch owner Dennis "Dr. D" Hartman go ballistic. The native Santa Barbaran says his store is dedicated to "people who know the difference between vinyl and CDs. I got everything—especially folk, rock and rhythm and blues—from '63 to '93, except punk, rap, heavy metal, and garbage."

Hartman, who's been in the record biz in Santa Barbara since 1980, carries several thousand records, one of the largest inventories in the state. Some albums are collector's items and are priced accordingly, but most can be obtained for $4, three for $10, even twenty-five or more for $2 apiece.

Morninglory Music

1218 State Street

966-0266

Monday-Thursday 10-10; Friday-Saturday 10-11 p.m.; Sunday 10-6

Morninglory Music has the latest titles in rock, blues, metal jazz and classical. Best bargains are in the store's generous selection of used compact discs, $4.99–$8.99. Look for the "USED, guaranteed to sound like new" stickers on old or newer favorites and take home CDs at lots less than new prices.

A Round-Up of Exceptional Annual Sales

"Apparel Designer Zone" Sales

Earl Warren Showgrounds

Four times a year save 50 to 90 percent off retail price of name-brand new merchandise—Esprit, Polo, DKNY, Guess and more—offered at top department stores. Admission is free, but parking at the showgrounds is $1.

Beachside Festival

Second weekend of July

Outlet District off Lower State Street

CASH (Capitalists Against Suffering & Hunger), brainstorm of Milan and Georgeana Melvin, is a volunteer project benefitting Tibetan and El Salvadoran refugees. CASH's annual sale, dubbed "The Beachside Festival," offers first-quality clothing, shoes, and accessories donated from their friends in the garment business locally and nationally. This festival, modelled after a Moroccan street bazaar, takes over a couple short blocks in the city's outlet district off lower State Street.

Channel Paper Company's Giant Warehouse Sale

26 South Salsipuedes Street

963-1981

The annual spring clean-up at Channel Paper is the time to stock up on office and school supplies, cases of paper products–and lots more. Many items sell at cost; others at discounts up to 50 percent.

Junior League Rummage Sale

Earl Warren Showgrounds

All year 'round, the Junior League collects donated goods to sell at their November sale. Furniture, collectibles, and items of all shapes and sizes are available at this wonderful rummage sale held at the Earl Warren Showgrounds, Las Positas and 101. Free admission; parking at the showgrounds is $1.

Planned Parenthood Book Sale

Every fall, Planned Parenthood holds its book sale to raise money to support low-income individuals and family planning services. Thousands of books are collected throughout the year, and they're offered for sale at bargain prices—most ranging from fifty cents to ten dollars. The event is held downtown at various locations, and is always well-advertised in advance.

Police Auction

Santa Barbara Police Department
215 East Figueroa Street

Twice a year, in June and December, the Santa Barbara Police Department property department unloads its miscellaneous unclaimed or non-returnable property. Items offered at the auctions may include jewelry, clothing, flashlights, lots of bicycles and even a dinghy or two. It's a fun time, with police officers serving as auctioneers, and bidding starting at $1. View the items from 10 to 11 a.m.; auction begins at 11 a.m.. Notices for the semi-annual events appear in local press for a week before the auction.

The Yes Store

During the holiday season, a shop opens downtown each year for just a few weeks. Filled with locally created artwork, photographs, sculpture, jewelry, specialty clothing, and imaginative gifts of all types, it's a must-visit on your holiday shopping tour of town. You may just be able to pick out something original for everyone on your list for one-stop shopping with a flair! Watch for notices in November newspapers for location and hours.

Bargain Basement Shopping

Santa Barbara Swap Meet

907 South Kellogg Avenue (Goleta)

964-9050

Sundays 7-3

Located at the Twin Screens drive-in, the Santa Barbara Swap Meet is Middle America, Southern California-style. Salsa rhythms punctuate the air; assorted merchandise offered for sale ranges from junk to treasures; there's inexpensive produce, brightly colored clothing and odd furniture, car parts and ancient-looking plumbing and carpentry tools. Admission is $1 per person, and worth the price, if only for the cultural experience.

Thrift Shops

There are many thrift shops doing business in Santa Barbara; most are run by charities to benefit their good works (although the overhead of running the shops takes a good bite out of the proceeds). These shops are crammed full of clothes, household items, furniture, and the like—ranging from almost new to almost worn out—usually at very inexpensive prices. In most cases, as the saying goes, you get what you pay for. You might possibly find something special, but it's going to take a lot of looking. Look in the Yellow Pages under "Thrift Stores" for locations and phone numbers. (Insider's Tip: The best shop in town is generally considered to be Alpha Thrift, currently located at 302 West Carrillo Street.)

Used Bookstores

Santa Barbara not only boasts more than its share of excellent independent bookstores (notably Earthling and Chaucer's), it also finds room for an array of used bookstores and a handful of antiquarian dealers as well. Bookselling is a touchy subject these days, with the expansionist chain superstores attempting to bury neighborhood independents; in general, I support buying books from neighborhood independents. When titles are out-of-print or especially difficult to locate, try a used bookshop. (One of the largest and most complete is **The Book Den**, 11 East Anapamu Street.)

Transportation

Almost-Free Shuttle

The formerly free ride is still a bargain at only a quarter

Hop an open-air electric shuttle and conserve energy in two ways—yours and fossil fuels! Route extends from Stearns Wharf up State Street to Sola, fourteen blocks away, and also from Stearns Wharf along the waterfront to the zoo. Hours vary by season; in summer the shuttle operates Sunday through Thursday 10 a.m. to 5 p.m.; later on Friday and Saturday. The shuttle stops at marked stops on every block on State Street, and passes every 10–20 minutes during the week, every 8–15 minutes on weekends.

MTD Bus Service

The centrally located Downtown Transit Center (at Chapala and Carrillo, one block west of the 1000 block of State Street), is the depot for the Metropolitan Transit District. Bus routes take riders to the far reaches of Goleta and Montecito, the beach and UCSB, for just seventy-five cents. Pick up a copy of "The Bus Book" for detailed route information, or call 683-3702.

Santa Barbara Trolley Company

This private company provides a narrated tour of the town for $4 for adults and $2 for children. The open-air trolley leaves Stearns Wharf every 90 minutes starting at 10 a.m. Call 965-0353.

A Word About Parking

On-street parking in the downtown district is 90 minutes except where indicated otherwise. Believe it! The city employs a fleet of very efficient parking enforcement officers who chalk tires and write tickets to raise money for the city.

These officers are dedicated workers, rigorous and punctual. If you don't want an ticket (no bargain at $20 or more), don't be tempted to overstay your time limit for even a few minutes. Note: Sundays are free, but not holidays; I've been ticketed on Fourth of July and Christmas Eve!

If you prefer not to press your luck, park in a lot. There are more than a dozen public parking lots located downtown; all city-owned lots offer 90 minutes free, $1 per hour afterward. Rates are in effect Monday through Saturday 7:30 a.m. through 7:30 p.m.; Sundays are free, but not holidays.

Parking on Stearns Wharf

Here are the most expensive parking rates in town— $2 an hour or any part of an hour. You can get two hours free parking with a validation and a minimum ($3) purchase from a shop or restaurant on the wharf. A better deal: park at any city lot for the first 90 minutes and either walk or take the shuttle to the wharf, or better yet, park anywhere but the wharf on Sunday without charge.

Gas

"Fill up before you get here," is the best advice for the motorist looking for bargain fuel. Santa Barbarans heading south on Highway 101 to Ventura or the great metropolis beyond invariably fill up or top their tanks on the return trip at one of a hundred stations between the north San Fernando Valley and Ventura. Simply put, there's no cheap gas in Santa Barbara; however, three stations consistently have cheaper gas than their civic counterparts:

JR's Gas on the Mesa

1905 Cliff Drive
Daily 7 a.m. to 9 p.m.

Over the hill from town on the corner of Carrillo Boulevard and Shoreline Drive. Surely it's the sweetest smelling gas station around: A flower stand perfumes one side of the station, a fruit and vegetable stand (Mesa Produce) the other, all cooled by an ocean breeze. Instead of suffering the soda pop and year-old candy bars featured at most gas station mini-marts, you can step into JR's service bay turned produce stand and get some healthy road food at low prices.

JR's has low prices (same for cash or credit cards) on gas. Pay cash and take advantage of JR's seasonal specials: ie. buy eight or more gallons of super unleaded and get a free box of strawberries.

Thrifty Gas

4069 State Street

964-9384

open 24 hours

Every gas pump has a sign atop it promising a bargain for items ranging from gum to STP. The real bargain, though, is the gas prices, about a nickel to a dime or more a gallon cheaper than other stations; in fact, the prices are lower than those of the Thrifty Gas on Milpas Street.

To gas-up, you'll have to put up with the station's you-can't-get-there-from-here upper Upper State Street location, which thwarts left turns near the station and requires U-turns past the station; however, if you happen to be heading south on 101, Thrifty Gas is conveniently situated right next to the on-ramp.

World Gas

2837 De la Vina

Monday through Saturday 6 a.m. to 10 p.m.; Sunday 7 a.m. to 10 p.m.

Sunday

A no-frills refueling stop. Definitely not a service station or particularly pleasant place to go, but it does boast some of very cheapest gas prices in town.

Maps

The Auto Club's "Cities of Santa Barbara County" ($2.95), free to AAA members, is a good map, and easy-to-obtain for visitors planning a trip to Santa Barbara. Unfortunately, the 1993 edition downsized the scale of Santa Barbara, making navigation difficult for the far-sighted and passenger-navigators.

True tightwads will photocopy the phone book's Downtown Santa Barbara map, which is good as far as it goes—central downtown.

Santa Barbara Conference & Visitor Bureau gives out a brochure entitled "Santa Barbara Things to See & Do"; it highlights tourist destinations, the downtown and waterfront areas.

Car Rental

U-Save Auto Rental

510 Anacapa Street

963-3499

Monday-Friday 8-5:30; weekends 9-1:00

A no-frills operation offering low-cost rentals on late-model compact ($19.95 a day) and mid-size ($24.95 a day) cars. Weekly and monthly rates are available; free pick-up and delivery.

Walking

Like most Mediterranean cities, Santa Barbara is a great place to walk. Mild weather, beautiful scenery, interesting neighborhoods, wonderful people watching; just put on your shoes, pick up a map, and start strolling. Best way to see, get to know a city is up-close and personal, one step at a time—and it's free! (Note: The author has an admitted bias for seeing Santa Barbara on foot; she and co-author John McKinney wrote *Walk Santa Barbara: City Strolls & County Rambles*, HarperWest 1994.)

Accommodations

With mid-week summer rates near the beach averaging about $100 per night, the only inexpensive place to stay in Santa Barbara is with a friend or relative. Yes, there are three outlets of America's cheap chain, but they're virtually always booked, and their prices are higher in Santa Barbara than in any of their other locations in the nation. (When I inquired the reason from one Motel 6 innkeeper she simply rolled her eyes, and said, "Yes, my dear, this is Santa Barbara.")

There are a couple of reservation services available in town that provide information free to callers: **Accommodations** (locally 687-9191; out-of-town 1-800-292-2222) and **Hot Spots** (locally 564-1637; out-of-town 1-800-793-7666). Hot Spots also provides walk-in services at their location at 36 State Street.

In winter months, the Santa Barbara Conference & Visitors Bureau promotes a program called "Nights in Paradise." Various hoteliers offer package deals with at least one free night; considering Santa Barbara's mild winters, November through March is a great time to stay and save. For more information, call locally 966-9222; out-of-town 1-800-927-4688.

For those who want to rough-it, there are four state park campgrounds nearby: Refugio, El Capitan, and Gaviota State beaches to the north, and Carpinteria State Beach to the south. For reservations, call MISTIX at 1-800-444-PARK.

Index

Other Titles from
Pacific Books & EZ Nature Books

Little Gray Whale Pocket Guide
Central Coast Wild Flowers
Wildlife Watchers Guide to San Luis Obispo
California Indian Watercraft
The Chumash People
California's Chumash Indians
Rock Paintings of the Chumash
From Fingers to Finger Bowls
Cabrillo
The Life & Times of Fr. Junípero Serra
San Luis Obispo Mission Cut-Out-and-Color Book
Mountain Biking The Central Coast
Bicycle San Luis Obispo County
Fog and Sun, Sea and Stone
Sentinels of Solitude
Making the Most of San Luis Obispo
Ventura Companion
Santa Barbara Secrets & Sidetrips
Santa Barbara: A Photo Essay
Mountains of Fire
Hearst's Dream

To order *The Santa Barbara Bargain Book*
by mail, please send $7.95 plus applicable sales tax to:

Pacific Books
Post Office 3562
Santa Barbara, CA 93130

Suggestions for Future Editions

Company Name _____

Address _____

Phone _____

Hours _____

Description of products and services _____

_____

_____

_____

Submitted by _____

Address _____

Phone _____

Send to Pacific Books
Post Office Box 3562
Santa Barbara, California 93130